A Gift For:

_____

From:

_____

Date:

_____

All Scripture quotations in this book are from the *Holy Bible,* New King James Version (NKJV)
© 1979, 1980, 1982, 1992, 2005 by Thomas Nelson, Inc. Used by permission.

www.thomasnelson.com

Cover and interior designed by Robin Black, Blackbird Creative LLC

ISBN-10:1-4041-0535-2
ISBN-13: 978-1-4041-0535-5

Printed in the United States

God's Guiding Touch

for MOTHERS

THOMAS NELSON
Since 1798

x

NASHVILLE DALLAS MEXICO CITY RIO DE JANEIRO BEIJING

Table of Contents

Give unto the LORD, O you mighty ones,
Give unto the LORD glory and strength.
Give unto the LORD the glory due to His name;
Worship the LORD in the beauty of holiness.

PSALM 29:1–2

Oh come,
let us worship and bow down;
Let us kneel before the LORD our Maker.
For He is our God,
And we are the people of His pasture,
And the sheep of His hand.

PSALM 95:6–7

Then you will call upon Me
and go and pray to Me,
and I will listen to you.
And you will seek Me and find Me,
when you search for Me
with all your heart.

JEREMIAH 29:12–13

Seek the LORD and His strength;
Seek His face evermore!
Remember His marvelous works which He has done,
His wonders, and the judgments of His mouth,

1 CHRONICLES 16:11–12

"*B*ut the hour is coming, and now is,
when the true worshipers will
worship the Father in spirit and truth;
for the Father is seeking such to worship Him.
God is Spirit, and those who worship Him
must worship in spirit and truth."

JOHN 4:23–24

*T*hus I will bless You while I live;
I will lift up my hands in Your name.
My soul shall be satisfied as with marrow and fatness,
And my mouth shall praise You with joyful lips.

PSALM 63:4–5

"If you love Me, keep My commandments."

JOHN 14:15

"Whoever comes to Me, and hears My sayings and does them, I will show you whom he is like: He is like a man building a house, who dug deep and laid the foundation on the rock. And when the flood arose, the stream beat vehemently against that house, and could not shake it, for it was founded on the rock. But he who heard and did nothing is like a man who built a house on the earth without a foundation, against which the stream beat vehemently; and immediately it fell. And the ruin of that house was great."

LUKE 6:47–49

Furthermore,
we have had human fathers who
corrected us, and we paid them respect.
Shall we not much more readily be in
subjection to the Father of spirits
and live? For they indeed for a few
days chastened us as seemed best
to them, but He for our profit,
that we may be partakers
of His holiness.

HEBREWS 12:9–10

"And when you pray,
you shall not be like
the hypocrites. For they love
to pray standing in the synagogues
and on the corners of the streets,
that they may be seen by men.
Assuredly, I say to you, they have their reward.
But you, when you pray,
go into your room, and when
you have shut your door,
pray to your Father who is
in the secret place; and your
Father who sees in secret
will reward you openly."

MATTHEW 6:5–6

12

Let us therefore come boldly
to the throne of grace,
that we may obtain mercy and
find grace to help in time of need.

HEBREWS 4:16

Give ear, O LORD, to my prayer;
And attend to the voice of my supplications.
In the day of my trouble I will call upon You,
For You will answer me.

PSALM 86:6–7

13

*Y*ou will make your prayer to Him,
He will hear you,
And you will pay your vows.
You will also declare a thing,
And it will be established for you;
So light will shine on your ways.

JOB 22:27–28

"For the Holy Spirit
will teach you in that very hour
what you ought to say."
LUKE 12:12

"But the Helper, the Holy Spirit,
whom the Father will send in My name,
He will teach you all things, and bring
to your remembrance all things
that I said to you."
JOHN 14:26

15

For what man knows the things of a man except
the spirit of the man which is in him? Even so no one
knows the things of God except the Spirit of God.
Now we have received, not the spirit of the world,
but the Spirit who is from God, that we might know the
things that have been freely given to us by God.
These things we also speak, not in words which man's
wisdom teaches but which the Holy Spirit teaches,
comparing spiritual things with spiritual.

1 CORINTHIANS 2:11–13

But if the Spirit of Him who raised Jesus from the dead dwells in you, He who raised Christ from the dead will also give life to your mortal bodies through His Spirit who dwells in you. . . . The Spirit Himself bears witness with our spirit that we are children of God, and if children, then heirs—heirs of God and joint heirs with Christ, if indeed we suffer with Him, that we may also be glorified together. . . . Likewise the Spirit also helps in our weaknesses. For we do not know what we should pray for as we ought, but the Spirit Himself makes intercession for us with groanings which cannot be uttered.

ROMANS 8:11, 16–18, 26

*P*raise the LORD!
Praise the LORD, O my soul!
While I live I will praise the LORD;
I will sing praises to my God while I have my being.

PSALM 146:1–2

*B*ecause Your lovingkindness is better than life,
My lips shall praise You.
Thus I will bless You while I live;
I will lift up my hands in Your name.
My soul shall be satisfied as with marrow and fatness,
And my mouth shall praise You with joyful lips.

PSALM 63:3–5

18

*P*raise the LORD!
Oh, give thanks to the LORD,
for He is good!
For His mercy endures forever.
Who can utter the
mighty acts of the LORD?
Who can declare
all His praise?

PSALM 106:1–2

*P*raise the LORD!
Praise, O servants of the LORD,
Praise the name of the LORD!
Blessed be the name of the LORD
From this time forth and forevermore!
From the rising of the sun to its going down
The LORD's name is to be praised.

PSALM 113:1–3

20

*Y*ou will keep him in perfect peace,
Whose mind is stayed on You,
Because he trusts in You.
Trust in the LORD forever,
For in YAH, the LORD, is everlasting strength.

ISAIAH 26:3–4

*B*ut the salvation of the righteous is from the LORD;
He is their strength in the time of trouble.
And the LORD shall help them and deliver them;
He shall deliver them from the wicked,
And save them,
Because they trust in Him.

PSALM 37:39–40

The LORD is on my side;
I will not fear.
What can man do to me? . . .
It is better to trust in the LORD
Than to put confidence in man.

PSALM 118:6, 8

In You, O LORD, I put my trust;
Let me never be put to shame. . . .
For You are my hope, O Lord GOD;
You are my trust from my youth. . . .
Let my mouth be filled with Your praise
And with Your glory all the day.

PSALM 71:1, 5, 8

*B*ehold, the Lord GOD shall come with a strong hand,
And His arm shall rule for Him;
Behold, His reward is with Him,
And His work before Him.

ISAIAH 40:10

*H*is work is honorable and glorious,
And His righteousness endures forever.
He has made His wonderful works to be remembered;
The LORD is gracious and full of compassion.

PSALM 111:3–4

For God has not given us a spirit of fear,
but of power and of love and of a sound mind.
Therefore do not be ashamed of the testimony of our Lord,
nor of me His prisoner, but share with me in
the sufferings for the gospel according to the
power of God, who has saved us and called us with a
holy calling, not according to our works,
but according to His own purpose and grace which was
given to us in Christ Jesus before time began.

2 TIMOTHY 1:7–9

25

"Come to Me, all you who labor
and are heavy laden,
and I will give you rest.
Take My yoke upon you and
learn from Me,
for I am gentle and lowly in heart,
and you will find rest for your souls.
For My yoke is easy and
My burden is light."

MATTHEW 11:28–30

Be anxious for nothing,
but in everything
by prayer and supplication,
with thanksgiving, let your
requests be made known to God;
and the peace of God,
which surpasses all understanding,
will guard your hearts and minds
through Christ Jesus.

PHILIPPIANS 4:6–7

As for me, I will call upon God,
And the LORD shall save me.
Evening and morning and at noon
I will pray, and cry aloud,
And He shall hear my voice.

PSALM 55:16–17

Now this is the confidence that we have in Him,
that if we ask anything according to His will, He hears us.
And if we know that He hears us, whatever we ask,
we know that we have the petitions
that we have asked of Him.

1 JOHN 5:14–15

This Book of the Law shall not depart from
your mouth, but you shall meditate in it day and night,
that you may observe to do according to all that
is written in it. For then you will make your
way prosperous, and then you will have good success.

JOSHUA 1:8

The LORD will command
His lovingkindness in the daytime,
And in the night His song
shall be with me—
A prayer to the God of my life.

PSALM 42:8

The law of the LORD is perfect,
converting the soul;
The testimony of the LORD is sure, making wise the simple;
The statutes of the LORD are right, rejoicing the heart;
The commandment of the LORD is pure,
enlightening the eyes . . .
More to be desired are they than gold,
Yea, than much fine gold;
Sweeter also than honey and the honeycomb.

PSALM 19:7–8, 10

O God, You are my God;
Early will I seek You;
My soul thirsts for You;
My flesh longs for You
In a dry and thirsty land
Where there is no water.

PSALM 63:1

I love those who love me,
And those who seek me diligently
will find me.

PROVERBS 8:17

I sought the LORD,
and He heard me,
And delivered me from all my fears.

PSALM 34:4

*S*eek the LORD and His strength;
Seek His face evermore!
Remember His marvelous works which He has done,
His wonders,
and the judgments of His mouth,

1 CHRONICLES 16:11–12

In You, O LORD, I put my trust;
Let me never be put to shame.
Deliver me in Your righteousness,
and cause me to escape;
Incline Your ear to me, and save me. . . .
For You are my hope, O Lord GOD;
You are my trust from my youth.

PSALM 71:1–2, 5

The LORD shall preserve you from all evil;
He shall preserve your soul.
The LORD shall preserve your going out
and your coming in
From this time forth, and even forevermore.

PSALM 121:7–8

*G*race and peace be multiplied to you in the
knowledge of God and of Jesus our Lord, as His divine
power has given to us all things that pertain to life
and godliness, through the knowledge of Him who called
us by glory and virtue, by which have been given to us
exceedingly great and precious promises, that through these
you may be partakers of the divine nature, having escaped
the corruption that is in the world through lust.

2 PETER 1:2–4

*I*t is better to trust in the LORD
Than to put confidence in man.

PSALM 118:8

*There is therefore now
no condemnation to those who are in Christ Jesus,
who do not walk according to the flesh,
but according to the Spirit.
For the law of the Spirit of life in Christ Jesus
has made me free from the law
of sin and death.*

ROMANS 8:1–2

*If we confess our sins, He is faithful
and just to forgive us our sins and
to cleanse us from all unrighteousness.*

1 JOHN 1:9

35

Now whom you forgive anything, I also forgive.
For if indeed I have forgiven anything,
I have forgiven that one for your sakes in the presence
of Christ, lest Satan should take advantage of us;
for we are not ignorant of his devices.

2 CORINTHIANS 2:10–11

And the Lord will deliver me from every
evil work and preserve me for His heavenly kingdom.
To Him be glory forever and ever. Amen!

2 TIMOTHY 4:18

36

"*I* am the vine,
you are the branches.
He who abides in Me,
and I in him, bears much fruit;
for without Me you can do nothing. . . .
You did not choose Me,
but I chose you
and appointed you that
you should go and bear fruit,
and that your fruit should remain,
that whatever you ask
the Father in My name
He may give you."

JOHN 15:16

O God, You are my God;
Early will I seek You; my soul thirsts for You;
My flesh longs for You in a dry and thirsty land
Where there is no water.
So I have looked for You in the sanctuary,
To see Your power and Your glory. . . .
My soul shall be satisfied as with marrow and fatness,
And my mouth shall praise You with joyful lips. . . .
Because You have been my help,
Therefore in the shadow of Your wings I will rejoice.

PSALM 63:1–2, 5, 7

I will instruct you and teach you
in the way you should go;
I will guide you with My eye.

PSALM 32:8

"*If* anyone serves Me, let him follow Me;
and where I am, there My servant will be also.
If anyone serves Me, him My Father will honor."

JOHN 12:26

Command those who are rich in this present age
not to be haughty, nor to trust in uncertain riches but
in the living God, who gives us richly all things to enjoy. Let
them do good, that they be rich in good works,
ready to give, willing to share, storing up for
themselves a good foundation for the time to come,
that they may lay hold on eternal life.

1 TIMOTHY 6:17–19

But let each one examine his own work,
and then he will have rejoicing in himself alone,
and not in another. For each one shall
bear his own load. Let him who is taught the word
share in all good things with him who teaches. . . .
And let us not grow weary while doing good,
for in due season we shall reap if we do not lose heart.

GALATIANS 6:4–6, 9

"By this all will know that you are My disciples,
if you have love for one another."

JOHN 13:35

Now by this we know
that we know Him,
if we keep His commandments.
He who says, "I know Him," and does
not keep His commandments, is a liar,
and the truth is not in him.
But whoever keeps His word,
truly the love of God
is perfected in him.
By this we know that
we are in Him.

1 JOHN 2:3–5

*B*ut someone will say,
"You have faith, and I have works."
Show me your faith without your works,
and I will show you my faith by my works.
You believe that there is one God. You do well.
Even the demons believe—and tremble!
But do you want to know, O foolish man,
that faith without works is dead?
Was not Abraham our father justified by works
when he offered Isaac his son on the altar?
Do you see that faith was working together with his works,
and by works faith was made perfect?

JAMES 2:18–22

So then, my beloved brethren,
let every man be swift to hear, slow to speak,
slow to wrath; for the wrath of man does not produce
the righteousness of God. Therefore lay aside
all filthiness and overflow of wickedness,
and receive with meekness the implanted word,
which is able to save your souls. . . .
Pure and undefiled religion before God and
the Father is this: to visit orphans
and widows in their trouble, and to keep oneself
unspotted from the world.

JAMES 1:19–21, 27

Therefore, having been
justified by faith, we have peace
with God through our Lord Jesus Christ,
through whom also we have access
by faith into this grace in which we stand,
and rejoice in hope of the glory of God.
And not only that, but we also glory
in tribulations, knowing that tribulation
produces perseverance;
and perseverance, character;
and character, hope.

ROMANS 5:1–4

The LORD will
guide you continually,
And satisfy your soul in drought,
And strengthen your bones;
You shall be like a watered garden,
And like a spring of water,
whose waters do not fail.

ISAIAH 58:11

The LORD is near to those who have a broken heart,
And saves such as have a contrite spirit.
Many are the afflictions of the righteous,
But the LORD delivers him out of them all.

PSALM 34:18–19

"Come to Me, all you who labor and
are heavy laden, and I will give you rest.
Take My yoke upon you and learn from Me,
for I am gentle and lowly in heart,
and you will find rest for your souls."

MATTHEW 11:28–29

Beloved, do not think it strange
concerning the fiery trial which is to try you,
as though some strange thing happened to you;
but rejoice to the extent that you partake
of Christ's sufferings, that when
His glory is revealed, you may also
be glad with exceeding joy.

1 PETER 4:12–13

The fear of man brings a snare,
But whoever trusts in the LORD shall be safe.

PROVERBS 29:25

And He said to me,
"My grace is sufficient for you,
for My strength is made perfect in weakness."
Therefore most gladly I will rather
boast in my infirmities, that the power
of Christ may rest upon me.

2 CORINTHIANS 12:9

The LORD will perfect that which concerns me;
Your mercy, O LORD, endures forever;
Do not forsake the works of Your hands.

PSALM 138:8

My soul, wait silently
for God alone,
For my expectation is from Him.
He only is my rock and my salvation;
He is my defense;
I shall not be moved.
In God is my salvation and my glory;
The rock of my strength,
And my refuge, is in God.

PSALM 62:5–7

When you pass through the waters,
I will be with you;
And through the rivers,
they shall not overflow you.
When you walk through the fire,
you shall not be burned,
Nor shall the flame scorch you.

ISAIAH 43:2

Yea, though I walk through
the valley of the shadow of death,
I will fear no evil;
For You are with me;
Your rod and Your staff, they comfort me.

PSALM 23:4

He raises the poor out of the dust,
And lifts the needy out of the ash heap . . .
He grants the barren woman a home,
Like a joyful mother of children.
Praise the LORD!

PSALM 113:7, 9

You number my wanderings;
Put my tears into Your bottle;
Are they not in Your book?
When I cry out to You,
Then my enemies will turn back;
This I know, because God is for me.
In God (I will praise His word),
In the LORD (I will praise His word),
In God I have put my trust;
I will not be afraid.
What can man do to me?

PSALM 56:8–11

52

My brethren,
count it all joy when
you fall into various trials,
knowing that
the testing of your faith
produces patience.
But let patience have its
perfect work, that you may
be perfect and complete,
lacking nothing.

JAMES 1:2–4

Therefore be patient, brethren, until the coming
of the Lord. See how the farmer waits for the precious
fruit of the earth, waiting patiently for it until
it receives the early and latter rain. You also be patient.
Establish your hearts, for the coming of
the Lord is at hand.

JAMES 5:7–8

Wait on the LORD;
Be of good courage,
And He shall strengthen your heart;
Wait, I say, on the LORD!

PSALM 27:14

54

*B*ut those who wait
on the LORD
Shall renew their strength;
They shall mount up
with wings like eagles,
They shall run and
not be weary,
They shall walk and
not faint.

ISAIAH 40:31

LORD, I cry out to You;
Make haste to me!
Give ear to my voice when I cry out to You.
Let my prayer be set before You as incense,
The lifting up of my hands as the evening sacrifice.

PSALM 141:1–2

NOW godliness with contentment is great gain.
For we brought nothing into this world,
and it is certain we can carry nothing out.
And having food and clothing,
with these we shall be content.

1 TIMOTHY 6:6–8

But the wisdom that is from above is first pure,
then peaceable, gentle, willing to yield,
full of mercy and good fruits, without partiality
and without hypocrisy.

JAMES 3:17

I have fought the good fight,
I have finished the race, I have kept the faith.
Finally, there is laid up for me the
crown of righteousness,
which the Lord, the righteous Judge,
will give to me on that Day,
and not to me only but also to all
who have loved His appearing.

2 TIMOTHY 4:7–8

Cast your burden on the LORD,
And He shall sustain you;
He shall never permit
the righteous to be moved.

PSALM 55:22

He has not dealt with us according to our sins,
Nor punished us according to our iniquities.
For as the heavens are high above the earth,
So great is His mercy toward those who fear Him;
As far as the east is from the west,
So far has He removed our
transgressions from us.

PSALM 103:10–12

Trust in the LORD
with all your heart,
And lean not on your own
understanding;
In all your ways acknowledge Him,
And He shall direct your paths.

PROVERBS 3:5–6

Love bears all things,
believes all things,
hopes all things,
endures all things.

1 CORINTHIANS 13:7

*N*ow may our Lord Jesus Christ Himself,
and our God and Father,
who has loved us and given us
everlasting consolation
and good hope by grace
comfort your hearts
and establish you
in every good word and work.

2 THESSALONIANS 2:16–17

"*This* is My commandment, that you love one another
as I have loved you. Greater love has no one than this,
than to lay down one's life for his friends."

JOHN 15:12–13

*L*et brotherly love continue.
Do not forget to entertain strangers, for by so doing
some have unwittingly entertained angels.

HEBREWS 13:1–2

*H*e who covers a transgression seeks love,
But he who repeats a matter
separates friends.

PROVERBS 17:9

A friend loves at all times,
And a brother is born for adversity.

PROVERBS 17:17

*F*or as the body is one and has many members,
but all the members of that one body,
being many, are one body, so also is Christ. . . .
And if one member suffers,
all the members suffer with it; or if one member
is honored, all the members rejoice with it.

1 CORINTHIANS 12:12, 26

He has shown you,
O man, what is good;
And what does the LORD
require of you
But to do justly,
To love mercy,
And to walk humbly
with your God?

MICAH 6:8

"*Give*, and it will be given to you:
good measure, pressed down, shaken together,
and running over will be put into your bosom.
For with the same measure that you use,
it will be measured back to you."

LUKE 6:38

By this we know love,
because He laid down His life for us.
And we also ought to lay down our lives
for the brethren. But whoever has
this world's goods, and sees his brother in need,
and shuts up his heart from him,
how does the love of God
abide in him?

1 JOHN 3:16–17

*N*ot returning evil for evil or reviling for reviling,
but on the contrary blessing, knowing that
you were called to this,
that you may inherit a blessing.

1 PETER 3:9

*A*nd let us not grow weary
while doing good,
for in due season we shall reap
if we do not lose heart.

GALATIANS 6:9

65

"A new commandment I give to you,
that you love one another;
as I have loved you, that you also love one another.
By this all will know that you are My disciples,
if you have love for one another."

JOHN 13:34–35

"And whoever desires to be first among you,
let him be your slave—just as the Son of Man did not
come to be served, but to serve, and to give
His life a ransom for many."

MATTHEW 20:27–28

And whatever you do,
do it heartily, as to the Lord
and not to men,
knowing that from the Lord you
will receive the reward
of the inheritance;
for you serve the Lord Christ.
But he who does wrong
will be repaid
for what he has done,
and there is no partiality.

COLOSSIANS 3:23–25

As each one has received a gift,
minister it to one another, as good stewards of the
manifold grace of God. If anyone speaks,
let him speak as the oracles of God. If anyone ministers,
let him do it as with the ability which God supplies,
that in all things God may be glorified through
Jesus Christ, to whom belong the glory and the
dominion forever and ever. Amen.

1 PETER 4:10–11

He who does not love does not know God,
for God is love.

1 JOHN 4:8

*R*ejoice with those who rejoice,
and weep with those who weep.
Be of the same mind toward one another.
Do not set your mind on high things,
but associate with the humble.
Do not be wise
in your own opinion.

ROMANS 12:15–16

*T*herefore comfort each other
and edify one another, just as you also are doing.

1 THESSALONIANS 5:11

*T*herefore let us pursue the things
which make for peace and the
things by which one may edify another.

ROMANS 14:19

*A*nd let us consider one another in order
to stir up love and good works, not forsaking the
assembling of ourselves together, as is
the manner of some, but exhorting one another,
and so much the more as you see the Day approaching.

HEBREWS 10:24–25

*B*ut if we walk in the light
as He is in the light,
we have fellowship
with one another,
and the blood
of Jesus Christ His Son
cleanses us from all sin.

1 JOHN 1:7

Rejoice always, pray without ceasing,
in everything give thanks;
for this is the will of God
in Christ Jesus for you.

1 THESSALONIANS 5:16–18

"For the eyes of the LORD are on the righteous,
And His ears are open to their prayers;
But the face of the LORD is against those who do evil."
And who is he who will harm you
if you become followers
of what is good?

1 PETER 3:12–13

And take the helmet of salvation, and the
sword of the Spirit, which is the word of God;
praying always with all prayer and supplication in the
Spirit, being watchful to this end with all perseverance
and supplication for all the saints.

EPHESIANS 6:17–18

Now this is the confidence that we have in Him,
that if we ask anything according to His will, He hears us.
And if we know that He hears us, whatever we ask,
we know that we have the petitions
that we have asked of Him.

1 JOHN 5:14–15

I will praise You, O LORD,
with my whole heart;
I will tell of all Your marvelous works.
I will be glad and rejoice in You;
I will sing praise to Your name,
O Most High.

PSALM 9:1–2

I will sing of the mercies of the LORD forever;
With my mouth will I make known Your
faithfulness to all generations.

PSALM 89:1

I will delight myself
in Your statutes;
I will not forget Your word. . . .
Make me understand
the way of Your precepts;
So shall I meditate
on Your wonderful works.

PSALM 119:16, 27

And it will be said in that day:
"Behold, this is our God;
We have waited for Him, and He will save us.
This is the LORD;
We have waited for Him;
We will be glad and rejoice in His salvation."

ISAIAH 25:9

"The LORD your God in your midst,
The Mighty One, will save;
He will rejoice over you with gladness,
He will quiet you with His love,
He will rejoice over you
with singing."

ZEPHANIAH 3:17

The LORD is my shepherd; I shall not want.
He makes me to lie down in green pastures;
He leads me beside the still waters.
He restores my soul;
He leads me in the paths of righteousness
For His name's sake.
Yea, though I walk through the valley
of the shadow of death,
I will fear no evil;
For You are with me;
Your rod and Your staff, they comfort me.

PSALM 23:1–4

I will say of the LORD,
"He is my refuge and my fortress;
My God, in Him I will trust."
Surely He shall deliver you from the snare of the fowler
And from the perilous pestilence.
He shall cover you with His feathers,
And under His wings you shall take refuge;
His truth shall be your shield and buckler.

PSALM 91:2–4

And we have such trust through Christ toward God.

2 CORINTHIANS 3:4

The LORD is your keeper;
The LORD is your shade
at your right hand. . . .
The LORD shall preserve you
from all evil;
He shall preserve your soul.
The LORD shall preserve your
going out and your coming in
From this time forth,
and even forevermore.

PSALM 121:5, 7–8

*Let us hold fast the confession of our hope
without wavering, for He who promised is faithful.*

HEBREWS 10:23

*And having shod your feet
with the preparation of the gospel of peace;
above all, taking the shield of faith
with which you will be able to quench
all the fiery darts of the wicked one.*

EPHESIANS 6:15–16

For we walk by faith, not by sight.

2 CORINTHIANS 5:7

*B*ut you, beloved,
building yourselves up
on your most holy faith,
praying in the Holy Spirit,
keep yourselves in the love of God,
looking for the mercy
of our Lord Jesus Christ
unto eternal life.

JUDE 20–21

"*H*ave I not commanded you?
Be strong and of good courage; do not be afraid,
nor be dismayed, for the LORD your God
is with you wherever you go."

JOSHUA 1:9

81

"These things I have spoken to you,
that My joy may remain in you, and that your joy
may be full. This is My commandment,
that you love one another as I have loved you."

JOHN 15:11–12

Let us come before His presence with thanksgiving;
Let us shout joyfully to Him with psalms.

PSALM 95:2

Because Your lovingkindness
is better than life,
My lips shall praise You.
Thus I will bless You while I live;
I will lift up my hands in Your name.
My soul shall be satisfied as with
marrow and fatness,
And my mouth shall praise
You with joyful lips.

PSALM 63:3–5

*L*et the word of Christ dwell in you richly
in all wisdom, teaching and admonishing
one another in psalms and hymns and spiritual songs,
singing with grace in your hearts to the Lord.

COLOSSIANS 3:16

*T*here is therefore now no condemnation
to those who are in Christ Jesus,
who do not walk according to the flesh,
but according to the Spirit.
For the law of the Spirit of life in Christ Jesus
has made me free from the law of sin and death.

ROMANS 8:1–2

Teaching us that,
denying ungodliness
and worldly lusts,
we should live soberly, righteously,
and godly in the present age,
looking for the blessed hope
and glorious appearing
of our great God and Savior
Jesus Christ.

TITUS 2:12–13

I have been crucified with Christ; it is no longer
I who live, but Christ lives in me; and the life which I
now live in the flesh I live by faith in the Son of God,
who loved me and gave Himself for me.

GALATIANS 2:20

I will sing to the LORD as long as I live;
I will sing praise to my God while I have my being.
May my meditation be sweet to Him;
I will be glad in the LORD.

PSALM 104:33–34

86

The LORD is my light and my salvation; whom shall I fear?
The LORD is the strength of my life; of whom shall I be afraid?
When the wicked came against me to eat up my flesh,
My enemies and foes, they stumbled and fell.
Though an army may encamp against me,
My heart shall not fear;
Though war may rise against me, in this I will be confident.
One thing I have desired of the LORD, that will I seek:
That I may dwell in the house of the LORD
All the days of my life, to behold the beauty of the LORD,
And to inquire in His temple.
For in the time of trouble He shall hide me in His pavilion;
In the secret place of His tabernacle He shall hide me;
He shall set me high upon a rock.

PSALM 27:1–5

*N*o weapon formed against you shall prosper,
And every tongue which rises against you in judgment
You shall condemn.
This is the heritage of the servants of the LORD,
And their righteousness is from Me,"
Says the LORD.

ISAIAH 54:17

"*I* cry out to the LORD with my voice;
With my voice to the LORD I make my supplication.
I pour out my complaint before Him;
I declare before Him my trouble.

PSALM 142:1–2

The LORD is your keeper;
The LORD is your shade
at your right hand.
The sun shall not strike you by day,
Nor the moon by night.
The LORD shall preserve you from all
evil; He shall preserve your soul.
The LORD shall preserve your going out
and your coming in
From this time forth,
and even forevermore.

PSALM 121:5–8

Now this is the confidence that we have in Him,
that if we ask anything according to His will,
He hears us. And if we know that He hears us,
whatever we ask, we know that we have
the petitions that we have asked of Him.

1 JOHN 5:14–15

"But seek first the kingdom of God
and His righteousness, and all these things
shall be added to you."

MATTHEW 6:33

*B*y which have been given to us exceedingly great
and precious promises, that through these you
may be partakers of the divine nature, having escaped
the corruption that is in the world through lust.
But also for this very reason, giving all diligence, add to
your faith virtue, to virtue knowledge, to knowledge
self–control, to self–control perseverance,
to perseverance godliness, to godliness brotherly kindness,
and to brotherly kindness love. For if these things are
yours and abound, you will be neither barren nor
unfruitful in the knowledge of our Lord Jesus Christ.

2 PETER 1:4–8

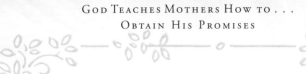

Let us hold fast the confession of our hope
without wavering,
for He who promised is faithful.

HEBREWS 10:23

" *For* with God nothing will be impossible."

LUKE 1:37

92

I have fought the good fight,
I have finished the race,
I have kept the faith.
Finally, there is laid up for me
the crown of righteousness,
which the Lord,
the righteous Judge, will give to me
on that Day, and not to me only
but also to all who have
loved His appearing.

2 TIMOTHY 4:7–8

*B*ut God, who is rich in mercy,
because of His great love with which He loved us,
even when we were dead in trespasses,
made us alive together with Christ
(by grace you have been saved),
and raised us up together, and made us sit together
in the heavenly places in Christ Jesus,
that in the ages to come He might show
the exceeding riches of His grace
in His kindness toward us in Christ Jesus.

EPHESIANS 2:4–7

Sing to the LORD with thanksgiving;
Sing praises on the harp to our God,
Who covers the heavens with clouds,
Who prepares rain for the earth,
Who makes grass to grow on the mountains.
He gives to the beast its food,
And to the young ravens that cry.
He does not delight in the strength of the horse;
He takes no pleasure in the legs of a man.
The LORD takes pleasure in those who fear Him,
In those who hope in His mercy.
Praise the LORD, O Jerusalem! Praise your God, O Zion!
For He has strengthened the bars of your gates;
He has blessed your children within you.

PSALM 147:7–13

For as many as are led by the Spirit of God,
these are sons of God. For you did not receive the spirit
of bondage again to fear, but you received the
Spirit of adoption by whom we cry out, "Abba, Father."
The Spirit Himself bears witness with our spirit
that we are children of God, and if children, then heirs—
heirs of God and joint heirs with Christ, if indeed
we suffer with Him, that we may also be glorified together.
For I consider that the sufferings of this present time
are not worthy to be compared with the glory
which shall be revealed in us.

ROMANS 8:14–18

But the wisdom
that is from above is first pure,
then peaceable,
gentle, willing to yield,
full of mercy and good fruits,
without partiality
and without hypocrisy.

JAMES 3:17

The fear of the LORD
is the beginning of wisdom;
A good understanding
have all those who do His commandments.
His praise endures forever.

PSALM 111:10

How much better to get
wisdom than gold!
And to get understanding
is to be chosen
rather than silver.

PROVERBS 16:16

Happy is the man who finds wisdom, and the man who
gains understanding; for her proceeds are better than the
profits of silver, and her gain than fine gold.
She is more precious than rubies, and all the things you may
desire cannot compare with her. Length of days is in
her right hand, in her left hand riches and honor.
Her ways are ways of pleasantness, and all her paths are
peace. She is a tree of life to those who
take hold of her, and happy are all who retain her.
The LORD by wisdom founded the earth;
by understanding He established the heavens;
by His knowledge the depths were broken up, and clouds
drop down the dew. My son, let them not depart
from your eyes—keep sound wisdom and discretion;
so they will be life to your soul and grace to your neck.

PROVERBS 3:13–22

Therefore, if anyone is in Christ, he is a new creation;
old things have passed away; behold, all things have
become new. Now all things are of God, who has reconciled
us to Himself through Jesus Christ, and has given us
the ministry of reconciliation, that is, that God was
in Christ reconciling the world to Himself,
not imputing their trespasses to them,
and has committed to us the word of reconciliation.
Now then, we are ambassadors for Christ, as though God
were pleading through us: we implore you on
Christ's behalf, be reconciled to God.

2 CORINTHIANS 5:17–20

*S*tand fast therefore
in the liberty by which Christ
has made us free,
and do not be entangled again
with a yoke of bondage.

GALATIANS 5:1

Create in me a clean heart, O God,
And renew a steadfast spirit within me.

PSALM 51:10

And you know that He was manifested
to take away our sins, and in Him there is no sin.
Whoever abides in Him does not sin. Whoever sins has
neither seen Him nor known Him. Little children,
let no one deceive you. He who practices righteousness
is righteous, just as He is righteous.

1 JOHN 3:5–7

This is the message which we have heard
from Him and declare to you, that God is light
and in Him is no darkness at all. If we say that we have
fellowship with Him, and walk in darkness,
we lie and do not practice the truth. But if we walk
in the light as He is in the light, we have fellowship with
one another, and the blood of Jesus Christ His Son
cleanses us from all sin. If we say that we have no sin,
we deceive ourselves, and the truth is not in us.
If we confess our sins, He is faithful and just to forgive us
our sins and to cleanse us from all unrighteousness.
If we say that we have not sinned,
we make Him a liar, and His word is not in us.

1 JOHN 1:5–10

The LORD builds up Jerusalem;
He gathers together the outcasts of Israel.
He heals the brokenhearted
And binds up their wounds. . . .
Great is our Lord, and mighty in power;
His understanding is infinite.
The LORD lifts up the humble;
He casts the wicked down to the ground. . . .
For He has strengthened the bars of your gates;
He has blessed your children within you.
He makes peace in your borders,
And fills you with the finest wheat.

PSALM 147:2–3, 5–6, 13–14

*C*asting all your care
upon Him, for He cares for you.
Be sober, be vigilant; because your
adversary the devil walks about like a
roaring lion, seeking whom he may
devour. Resist him, steadfast in the
faith, knowing that the same sufferings
are experienced by your brotherhood in
the world. But may the God of all
grace, who called us to His eternal
glory by Christ Jesus, after you
have suffered a while, perfect,
establish, strengthen,
and settle you.

1 PETER 5:7–11

I will bless the LORD at all times;
His praise shall continually be in my mouth.
My soul shall make its boast in the LORD;
The humble shall hear of it and be glad.
Oh, magnify the LORD with me,
And let us exalt His name together.
I sought the LORD, and He heard me,
And delivered me from all my fears. . . .
This poor man cried out, and the LORD heard him,
And saved him out of all his troubles.
The angel of the LORD encamps all around
those who fear Him, and delivers them.
Oh, taste and see that the LORD is good;
Blessed is the man who trusts in Him!

PSALM 34:1–8

Yet in all these things we are more than conquerors
through Him who loved us. For I am persuaded
that neither death nor life, nor angels nor principalities
nor powers, nor things present nor things to come, nor
height nor depth, nor any other created thing,
shall be able to separate us from the love of God
which is in Christ Jesus our Lord.

ROMANS 8:37–39

Then Jesus spoke to them again, saying,
"I am the light of the world.
He who follows Me shall not walk in darkness,
but have the light of life."

JOHN 8:12

The LORD is my light and my salvation; whom shall I fear? The LORD is the strength of my life; of whom shall I be afraid? . . . Though an army may encamp against me, my heart shall not fear; though war may rise against me, in this I will be confident. One thing I have desired of the LORD, that will I seek: That I may dwell in the house of the LORD all the days of my life, to behold the beauty of the LORD, and to inquire in His temple. For in the time of trouble He shall hide me in His pavilion . . . He shall set me high upon a rock. . . . Therefore I will offer sacrifices of joy in His tabernacle; I will sing, yes, I will sing praises to the LORD.

PSALM 27:1–6

The LORD shall judge the peoples;
Judge me, O LORD, according to my righteousness,
And according to my integrity within me.

PSALM 7:8

"If I have walked with falsehood,
Or if my foot has hastened to deceit,
Let me be weighed on honest scales,
That God may know my integrity.

JOB 31:5–6

Delight yourself also in the LORD,
And He shall give you the desires of your heart.
Commit your way to the LORD,
Trust also in Him,
And He shall bring it to pass.
He shall bring forth your righteousness as the light,
And your justice as the noonday.

PSALM 37:4–6

I will behave wisely in a perfect way. Oh, when will You come to me? I will walk within my house with a perfect heart. I will set nothing wicked before my eyes; I hate the work of those who fall away; It shall not cling to me. A perverse heart shall depart from me; I will not know wickedness. Whoever secretly slanders his neighbor, him I will destroy; The one who has a haughty look and a proud heart, him I will not endure. My eyes shall be on the faithful of the land, that they may dwell with me; he who walks in a perfect way, he shall serve me. He who works deceit shall not dwell within my house; He who tells lies shall not continue in my presence. Early I will destroy all the wicked of the land, that I may cut off all the evildoers from the city of the LORD.

PSALM 101:2–8

*B*ut, beloved, do not forget this one thing,
that with the Lord one day is as a thousand years,
and a thousand years as one day.
The Lord is not slack concerning His promise,
as some count slackness, but is longsuffering toward us,
not willing that any should perish
but that all should come to repentance.

2 PETER 3:8–9

*Y*et if anyone suffers as a Christian,
let him not be ashamed,
but let him glorify God in this matter.

1 PETER 4:16

112

He who covers his sins
will not prosper,
But whoever confesses and
forsakes them will have mercy.

PROVERBS 28:13

Blessed are those
who keep His testimonies,
Who seek Him
with the whole heart!

PSALM 119:2

Beloved, do not think it strange concerning
the fiery trial which is to try you, as though
some strange thing happened to you;
but rejoice to the extent that you partake
of Christ's sufferings, that when His glory is revealed,
you may also be glad with exceeding joy.

1 PETER 4:12–13

Hear me, O LORD, for Your lovingkindness is good . . .
And do not hide Your face from Your servant,
For I am in trouble; Hear me speedily.
Draw near to my soul, and redeem it;
Deliver me because of my enemies.

PSALM 69:16–18

114

Heal me, O LORD, and I shall be healed;
Save me, and I shall be saved, for You are my praise.

JEREMIAH 17:14

Yea, though I walk through the valley
of the shadow of death, I will fear no evil;
For You are with me;
Your rod and Your staff, they comfort me.

PSALM 23:4

For this is God,
Our God forever and ever;
He will be our guide even to death.

PSALM 48:14

*W*ho shall separate us from the love of Christ?
Shall tribulation, or distress, or persecution, or famine,
or nakedness, or peril, or sword? As it is written:
"For Your sake we are killed all day long;
We are accounted as sheep for the slaughter."
Yet in all these things we are more than conquerors through
Him who loved us. For I am persuaded that neither death
nor life, nor angels nor principalities nor powers, nor things
present nor things to come, nor height nor depth, nor any
other created thing, shall be able to separate us
from the love of God which is in
Christ Jesus our Lord.

ROMANS 8:35–39

116

And the Lord said, "Who then is that faithful and
wise steward, whom his master will make ruler
over his household, to give them their portion of food in
due season? Blessed is that servant whom his master
will find so doing when he comes. Truly, I say to you that
he will make him ruler over all that he has.

LUKE 12:42–44

And my God shall supply all your need
according to His riches in glory by Christ Jesus.

PHILIPPIANS 4:19

Listen, my beloved brethren: Has God not chosen the
poor of this world to be rich in faith and heirs of
the kingdom which He promised to those who love Him?

JAMES 2:5

Then He said to His disciples,
"Therefore I say to you, do not worry about your life,
what you will eat; nor about the body,
what you will put on. Life is more than food,
and the body is more than clothing.
Consider the ravens, for they neither sow nor reap,
which have neither storehouse nor barn;
and God feeds them.
Of how much more value are you
than the birds?"

LUKE 12:22–24

The righteous shall flourish
like a palm tree,
He shall grow like a cedar in Lebanon.
Those who are planted
in the house of the LORD
Shall flourish in the courts of our God.
They shall still bear fruit in old age;
They shall be fresh and flourishing,
To declare that the LORD is upright;
He is my rock,
and there is
no unrighteousness
in Him.

PSALM 92:12–15

119

But as for me, I trust in You, O LORD;
I say, "You are my God."
My times are in Your hand;
Deliver me from the hand of my enemies,
And from those who persecute me.

PSALM 31:14–15

For I know that my Redeemer lives,
And He shall stand at last on the earth;
And after my skin is destroyed, this I know,
That in my flesh I shall see God.

JOB 19:25–26

120

For none of us lives to himself, and no one dies to himself.
For if we live, we live to the Lord;
and if we die, we die to the Lord.
Therefore, whether we live or die, we are the Lord's.

ROMANS 14:7–8

The days of our lives are seventy years;
And if by reason of strength they are eighty years,
Yet their boast is only labor and sorrow;
For it is soon cut off, and we fly away. . . .
So teach us to number our days,
That we may gain a heart of wisdom. . . .
Oh, satisfy us early with Your mercy,
That we may rejoice and be glad all our days!

PSALM 90:10, 12, 14

121

I will both lie down in peace, and sleep;
For You alone, O LORD, make me dwell in safety.

PSALM 4:8

*T*he angel of the LORD encamps
all around those who fear Him,
And delivers them.

PSALM 34:7

*H*e who dwells in the secret place of the Most High
Shall abide under the shadow of the Almighty.
I will say of the LORD, "He is my refuge and my fortress;
My God, in Him I will trust."

PSALM 91:1–2

"Are not two sparrows
sold for a copper coin?
And not one of them falls to the
ground apart from your Father's will.
But the very hairs of your head are all
numbered. Do not fear therefore;
you are of more value than many sparrows."

MATTHEW 10:29–31

"Whoever listens to me will
dwell safely, and will be secure,
without fear of evil."

PROVERBS 1:33

For the mountains shall depart
And the hills be removed,
But My kindness shall not depart from you,
Nor shall My covenant of peace be removed,"
Says the LORD, who has mercy on you.

ISAIAH 54:10

All your children shall be taught by the LORD,
And great shall be the peace of your children.

ISAIAH 54:13

"No weapon formed against you shall prosper,
And every tongue which rises against you in judgment
You shall condemn.
This is the heritage of the servants of the LORD,
And their righteousness is from Me,"
Says the LORD.

ISAIAH 54:17

Not that I speak in regard to need,
for I have learned in whatever state I am, to be content:
I know how to be abased, and I know how to abound.
Everywhere and in all things I have learned both to be full
and to be hungry, both to abound and to suffer need.

PHILIPPIANS 4:11–12

125

*N*ow godliness with contentment is great gain.
For we brought nothing into this world,
and it is certain we can carry nothing out.
And having food and clothing,
with these we shall be content.

1 TIMOTHY 6:6–8

*T*he LORD will guide you continually,
And satisfy your soul in drought,
And strengthen your bones;
You shall be like a watered garden,
And like a spring of water,
whose waters do not fail.

ISAIAH 58:11

The LORD is your keeper;
The LORD is your shade
at your right hand.
The sun shall not strike you by day,
Nor the moon by night.
The LORD shall preserve you
from all evil;
He shall preserve your soul.
The LORD shall preserve your
going out and your coming in
From this time forth,
and even forevermore.

PSALM 121:5–8

But as it is written:
"Eye has not seen, nor ear heard,
Nor have entered into the heart of man
The things which God has prepared
for those who love Him."

1 CORINTHIANS 2:9